A COLLECTION OF PENTATONIC SONGS
compiled by Dr. ROBERT E. KERSEY

S.B.900

FOREWORD

This collection is a compilation of pentatonic songs. The natural chants and games of children and folk songs of all cultures demonstrate that the simplicity of songs without the complications of the half steps provides a sound and natural basis for developing musical literacy. Melodies can be recalled and sung with considerable accuracy when only the five tones without half steps are involved. Relationships are easily discovered and a basis upon which to expand into the complete diatonic scale can be firmly implanted.

Many teachers have discovered that a natural sequence exists and incorporated it into their teaching strategy. Children throughout the world have naturally used the descending minor third *sol - mi* for games, calling to pets or friends. For this reason, this should be the first interval to be memorized. The next step in the natural sequence is the addition of *la* - forming the familiar *sol - sol - mi - la - sol - mi* motif. With the addition of *re* and *do* the complete pentatonic scale is formed. The most notable teacher in developing this approach was Zoltán Kodály. He incorporated the use of hand signals with the movable *"do"*, giving the learner both a visual perception of the movement of sound and a physical involvement with the pitch direction. Some learn to "think" and "hear" with their hands.

This collection of songs is designed to provide supplementary material for teachers using the pentatonic approach. Songs based upon the tones *do - re - mi - sol - la* have been compiled under one cover so that sufficient practice material is readily available. At the beginning of each song a "key" with the movable clef provides a summary of the five tones used in that song. D - R - M - S - L are used to designate *do - re - mi - sol - la*. A line under a syllable abbreviation indicates the same syllable an octave lower; a line over a syllable abbreviation indicates the same syllable an octave higher.

Piano accompaniment has been deliberately omitted. The use of piano accompaniment has a tendency to establish a tonic-domina   relationship which inhibit the pentatonic approach to teaching music reading. After students have been firmly grounded in the pentatonic "skeleton," they can expand into the full diatonic scal with little difficulty.

TABLE OF CONTENTS

IT'S RAINING

GAME SONG

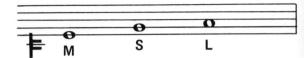

It's rain - ing, it's pour - ing, The old man is snor - ing, Went to bed and he bumped his head And he did - n't get up in the morn - ing.

RAIN, RAIN

GAME SONG

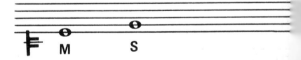

Rain, rain go a - way, Come a - gain some oth - er day.

S.B.900

DEE-DLE, DEE-DLE, DUMPLING

GAME SONG

Lively

Dee - dle, dee - dle, dump - ling, my son John,

Went to bed with his stock - ings on; One shoe off and

one shoe on, Dee-dle, dee - dle, dump- ling, my son John.

HOT CROSS BUNS

GAME SONG

Moderately

Hot cross buns! Hot cross buns!

One a pen - ny, two a pen - ny, Hot cross buns!

HUSH, LITTLE BABY
GAME SONG

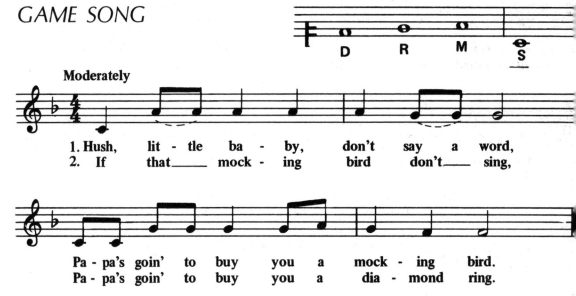

1. Hush, lit - tle ba - by, don't say a word,
2. If that mock - ing bird don't sing,

Pa - pa's goin' to buy you a mock - ing bird.
Pa - pa's goin' to buy you a dia - mond ring.

3. If that diamond ring turns brass,
   Papa's goin' to buy you a looking glass.

4. If that looking glass gets broke,
   Papa's goin' to buy you a billy goat.

5. If that billy goat gets bony,
   Papa's goin' to buy you a Shetland pony.

6. If that pony runs away,
   Papa's goin' to buy you a load of hay.

7. If that hay and cart turn over,
   Papa's goin' to buy you a dog named Rover.

8. If that big dog runs away,
   Papa'll get another one. Some fine day.

COUNTING SONG
GAME SONG

1. There were ten in the bed and the
2. There were nine in the bed and the

lit - tle one said, "Roll o - ver, roll o - ver!" So they
lit - tle one said, "Roll o - ver, roll o - ver!" So they

Last stanza

all rolled o - ver and one fell out. There were

all rolled o - ver and one fell out.

ten in the bed and the lit - tle one said, "Good night."

3.to 9.   There were eight, etc. (down to one).

10.   There was one in the bed and the little one said,
        "Roll over, roll over!"
        There was one in the bed and one jumped in.

11.to 18.   There were two, etc. (up to ten).

OLD BRASS WAGON

GAME SONG

D   R   M   S   L

1. Cir - cle to the left, Old Brass Wag - on,
2. Swing, Oh swing, Old Brass Wag - on,
3. Skip - ping all a - round, Old Brass Wag - on,

Cir - cle to the left, Old Brass Wag - on, Cir - cle to the left,
Swing, Oh, swing, Old Brass Wag - on, Swing, Oh, swing,
Skip-ping all a -round, Old Brass Wag - on, Skip-ping all a -round,

Old Brass Wag - on, You're the one, my dar - ling.
Old Brass Wag - on, You're the one, my dar - ling.
Old Brass Wag - on, You're the one, my dar - ling.

SONG TO THE SUN

ZUNI SONG

SKYE BOAT SONG

SCOTTISH FOLK SONG

Flowingly

Refrain

Speed, bon-nie boat, like a bird on the wing;

"On-ward," the sail-ors cry. Car-ry the lad that's

born to be king, O-ver the sea to Skye.

Verse

1. Loud the winds howl, loud the waves roar, Thun-der-clouds rend the
2. Tho' the waves leap, soft shall ye sleep, O-cean's a roy-al

air; Baf-fled, our foes stand by the shore;
bed. Rock'd in the deep, Flo-ra will keep

to Refrain

Fol-low they will not dare.
Watch by your wea-ry head.

3. Many's the lad fought on that day,
   Well the claymore could wield,
   When the nights came, silently lay
   Dead on Culloden's Field

   Refrain

4. Burn'd are our homes, exile and death
   Scatter the loyal men;
   Yet ere the sword cool in the sheath,
   Charlie will come again.

   Refrain

S.B.900

THE VILLAGE WATCHMAN

CANTONESE FOLK SONG

Rhythmically

1. Watch-man makes night's first round; Moth-er says, "What
2. Watch-man makes sec-ond round; Fa-ther says, "What
3. Watch-man makes night's third round; Sis-ter says, "What

is that sound?" Zing, zing, zing, hear mos-qui-toes
is that sound?" Gih, gih, gih, calls the mouse to
is that sound?" Mew, mew, mew, howls the cat out

sing; Hear them zing, zing, zing, zing, zing, zing, zing,
him; Hear him gih, gih, gih, gih, gih, gih, gih,
side; Hear him mew, mew, mew, mew, mew, mew, mew,

Zing, zing, zing, zing, zing, zing! _____
Gih, gih, gih, gih, gih, gih! _____
Mew, mew, mew, mew, mew, mew! _____

TURN THE GLASSES OVER
AMERICAN GAME SONG

Gaily

I've been to Haar - lem, I've been to Do - ver,

I've trav - eled this wide world all o - ver,

o - ver, o - ver, three times o - ver,

Drink what you have to drink and turn the glass - es o - ver,

Sail - ing east, sail - ing west, Sail - ing o - ver the

o - cean, Bet - ter watch out when the boat be - gins to rock,

Or you'll lose your girl in the o - cean.

S.B.900

MISTER RABBIT
AMERICAN FOLK SONG

Gaily

1. "Mis-ter Rab-bit, Mis-ter Rab-bit, Your ears are might-y long."
2. "Mis-ter Rab-bit, Mis-ter Rab-bit, You leave my cab-bage patch!"
3. "Mis-ter Rab-bit, Mis-ter Rab-bit, Your tail is might-y white!"

"Yes, in - deed,___ they're put on wrong."___
"Yes, in - deed,___ don't hook that latch!"___
"Yes, in - deed, I'm get-tin' out of sight!"___

JINGLE AT THE WINDOW
SINGING GAME

Gaily

Pass one win-dow, ti - de - o, Pass two win-dows,

ti - de - o, Pass three win - dows, ti - de - o,

Jin - gle at the win-dows, ti - de - o. Ti - de - o,

ti - de - o, Jin - gle at the win-dows, ti - de - o,

INDIAN WARRIOR

ARAPAHOE INDIAN MELODY

Rhythmically

I'm an In - dian war - ri - or, war - ri - or,
On my back a quiv - er, quiv - er,

Big Chief In - dian war - ri - or, war - ri - or.
Full of man - y ar - rows, ar - rows.

I'm an In - dian war - ri - or, war - ri - or,

Big Chief In - dian war - ri - or, war - ri - or,

Hi - ho! Hi -

ho! Hi!

(spoken)

S.B.900

THE SUNRISE CALL

ZUNI INDIAN SONG

AHRIRANG

KOREAN FOLK SONG

Moderately
Refrain

Ah - ri - rang, Ah - ri - rang, Ah - ri - ri - o,_____

As you pro - ceed_ a - long_ Ah - ri - ran pass,

1. You, my loved one, who me have_ for - sak - en,
2. Blue the sky with its myr - i - ad___ stars,___ so

to Refrain

Pain - ed be your feet_ at___ the___ end of a mile.
Sad - ness fills my heart_ with_ its___ myr - i - ad woes.

TONGO

POLYNESIAN

Moderately
Leader *Group* *Leader* *Group*

Ton - go_ Ton - go_ Jim - nee bye_ bye - oh Jim - nee bye_

bye - oh Ton - go___ Ton - go___ Oom ba de kim bye oh

Oom ba de kim bye oh Ooh - a lay, Ooh - a -

lay, Mah - le - ka - ah lo way. Mah - le - ka - ah lo way.

THE PURPLE BAMBOO

CHINESE FOLK SONG

1. See, I bring to you pur - ple bam - boo shoot,
2. You must try and grow like the bam - boo tall,

Now 'twill make a love - ly flute; But those lips so
Then those part -ing lips so small Soon will play the

small Can - not play at all On a love - ly
flute Made from bam -boo shoot; Sil - v'ry tunes will

Refrain

gold - en__ flute. Ee - tee - tee, Soon will come the
gen - tly__ fall.

hap - py day. day. My son the flute will play.

S.B.900

ROCK ISLAND LINE
RAILROAD WORK SONG

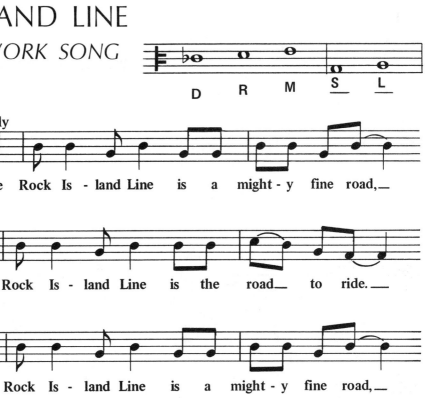

D   R   M   S   L

Rhythmically

Oh, the Rock Is - land Line is a might - y fine road, __

Oh, the Rock Is - land Line is the road__ to ride. __

Oh, the Rock Is - land Line is a might - y fine road, __

If you want to ride, you got to ride it like you find it,

Get your tick - et at the sta - tion on the Rock Is - land Line.

1. A   B   C   dou - ble   X   Y   Z,   Cat's in the
2. No - body cares for the rail - road man,   You're gon - na

cup - board but she can't see me. __
miss __ me __ when I'm gone. __

S.B.900

THE DERBY RAM

ENGLISH FOLK SONG

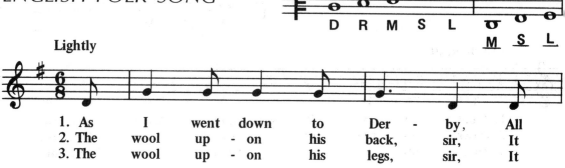

Lightly

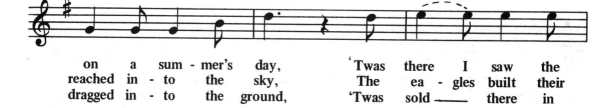

1. As I went down to Der - by, All
2. The wool up - on his back, sir, It
3. The wool up - on his legs, sir, It

on a sum - mer's day, 'Twas there I saw the
reached in - to the sky, The ea - gles built their
dragged in - to the ground, 'Twas sold there in

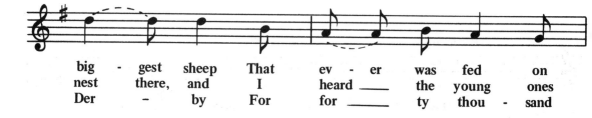

big - gest sheep That ev - er was fed on
nest there, and I heard the young ones
Der - by For for ty thou - sand

hay. } And sing tith - er - y i re -
cry.
pounds. }

oo - ry ann, Sing tith - er - y i o day.

4. The horns upon his head, sir,
   They reached unto the moon.
   A man went up in February
   And ne'er came down till June.
   And sing tithery . . . .

5. He had four feet to walk, sir,
   He had four feet to stand.
   And every foot he had, sir,
   It covered an acre of land.
   And sing tithery . . . .

THE LAND OF THE SILVER BIRCH

CANADIAN FOLK SONG

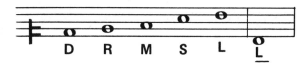

Rhythmically

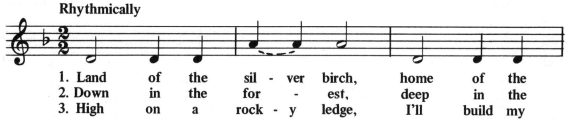

1. Land of the sil - ver birch, home of the
2. Down in the for - est, deep in the
3. High on a rock - y ledge, I'll build my

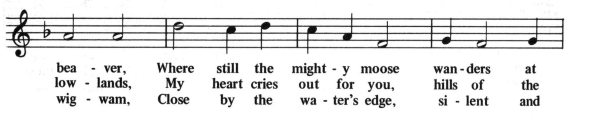

bea - ver, Where still the might - y moose wan - ders at
low - lands, My heart cries out for you, hills of the
wig - wam, Close by the wa - ter's edge, si - lent and

Refrain

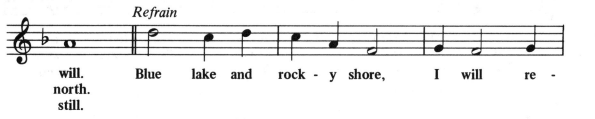

will. Blue lake and rock - y shore, I will re -
north.
still.

turn once more. Boom de de boom boom, Boom de de boom boom,

Boom de de boom boom, Boo - oo - oom.____

S.B.900

MY BIG BLACK DOG

ENGLISH PLAY SONG

Who - ev - er took my big black dog, I

wish they'd bring him back! He chased the big chicks

o - ver the fence and the lit - tle chicks thro' the

crack! The big chicks o - ver the fence and the

lit - tle chicks thro' the crack! Who - ev - er took my

big black dog, I wish they'd bring him back!

THE LONE STAR TRAIL
AMERICAN BALLAD

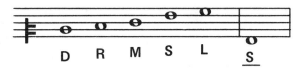

Lively

1. I___ start-ed on the trail___ on ___ June twen-ty
2. I'm___ up___ in the morn-ing be - fore day-
3. Oh, it's ba-con and___ beans most___ ev - 'ry___
4. With my knees___ in the sad-dle and my seat in the

third, I've been punch-ing Tex - as cat - tle on the Lone Star
light, And be - fore I go to sleep the yel - low moon shines
day, I'd___ just as soon be eat - ing tough old prai - rie ___
sky, I'll quit punch-ing Tex - as cat - tle in the sweet by and

Refrain

Trail. Sing-ing ki - yi - yip - py yip-py yay, yip-py
bright.
hay.
by.

yay, Sing-ing ki - yi - yip - py yip-py yay. _____

CAPE COD CHANTEY

AMERICAN SEA CHANTEY

Moderately

Solo

1. Glos' - ter girls they have no combs,
2. Glos' - ter boys they have no sleds,

Chorus ... *Solo*

Heave a - way, heave a - way! They comb their hair with
Heave a - way, heave a - way! They slide down hill on

Chorus

cod - fish bones, We're bound for South Aus - tral - ia.
cod - fish heads, We're bound for South Aus - tral - ia.

Refrain
(Chorus)

Heave a - way, my bul - ly, bul - ly, boys, Heave a - way,

heave a - way! Heave a - way, why don't you make a noise?

We're bound for South Aus - tral - ia.

SCRAPING UP SAND

FOLK SONG

D R M S L D S

Lively

1. Scrap-ing up the sand from the bot-tom of the sea,
2. Pick-ing up the pears that have fal-len from the tree,
3. Pick-ing out the weeds from the wa-ter-mel-on patch,

Shi - loh! Shi - loh! Scrap-ing up the sand from the
Shi - loh! Shi - loh! Pick-ing up the pears that have
Shi - loh! Shi - loh! Pick-ing out the weeds from the

bot-tom of the sea, Shi - loh! Li - za Jane!
fal-len from the tree, Shi - loh! Li - za Jane!
wa-ter-mel-on patch, Shi - loh! Li - za Jane!

Refrain

Oh, how I'll miss you! Oh, what a shame!

Oh, how I'll miss you! Bye, bye, Li - za Jane!

S.B.900

ROCKY MOUNTAIN
SOUTHERN FOLK SONG

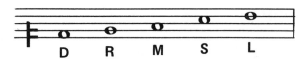

Lively

1. Rock - y moun- tain, rock - y moun-tain, rock - y moun - tain
2. Sun - ny val - ley, sun - ny val - ley, sun - ny val - ley
3. Storm - y o - cean, storm - y o - cean, storm - y o - cean

high,   When you're on that rock - y moun - tain,
low,   When you're in that sun - ny val - ley,
wide;   When you're on that deep blue sea, there's

Refrain

hang your head and cry!   Do, do,
sing it soft and slow.
no place you can hide.

do, do, do re - mem - ber me;

Do, do, do, do do, re - mem-ber me.

S.B.900

SING-A-LING-A-LING
AMERICAN CAMP SONG

Oh (John - ny Jones), we sing - a - ling - a - ling with
(substitute any name)

all our hearts to you; We hope there'll be some -

thing - a - ling - a - ling that we can do for

you. In au - tumn, win - ter, spring - a - ling - a ling, and

all the whole year through; We'll ring - a - ling - a - ling and

sing - a - ling - a - ling and ching - a - ling - a - ling for you.

S.B.900

CRAWDAD*
AMERICAN FOLK SONG

Lively

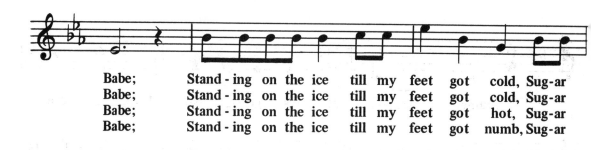

1. Stand-ing on the ice till my feet got cold, Sug-ar
2. Stand-ing on the ice till my feet got cold, Sug-ar
3. Stand-ing on the ice till my feet got hot, Sug-ar
4. Stand-ing on the ice till my feet got numb, Sug-ar

Babe; Stand-ing on the ice till my feet got cold, Sug-ar
Babe; Stand-ing on the ice till my feet got cold, Sug-ar
Babe; Stand-ing on the ice till my feet got hot, Sug-ar
Babe; Stand-ing on the ice till my feet got numb, Sug-ar

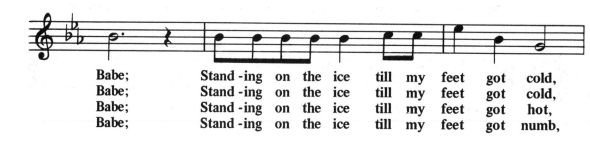

Babe; Stand-ing on the ice till my feet got cold,
Babe; Stand-ing on the ice till my feet got cold,
Babe; Stand-ing on the ice till my feet got hot,
Babe; Stand-ing on the ice till my feet got numb,

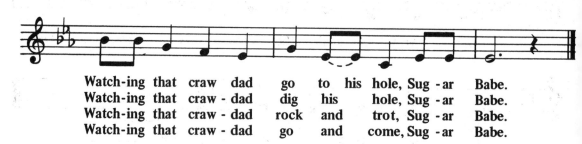

Watch-ing that craw dad go to his hole, Sug-ar Babe.
Watch-ing that craw-dad dig his hole, Sug-ar Babe.
Watch-ing that craw-dad rock and trot, Sug-ar Babe.
Watch-ing that craw-dad go and come, Sug-ar Babe.

A crawdad (crayfish) is a very small fresh-water lobster.

GARDEN HYMN
SOUTHERN FOLK SONG

Flowingly

The ___ Lord in - to ___ His gar - den comes. ___ The spic - es yield a rich ___ per - fume. The ___ lil - ies grow ___ and thrive, ___ the lil - ies grow ___ and thrive. ___ Re - fresh - ing show'rs of grace di - vine From ___ Je - sus flow to ev - ry vine And ___ make the dead ___ re - vive, ___ And make the dead ___ re - vive. ___

S.B.900

28

JENNIE JENKINS

EARLY AMERICAN SONG

Brightly

Boys

1. Will you wear white, O my dear, O my dear?
2. Will you wear red, O my dear, O my dear?

Oh, will you wear white Jen-nie Jen - kins?
Oh, will you wear red Jen-nie Jen - kins?

Girls

I won't wear white, for the col - or's too bright,
I won't wear red, it's the col - or'v my head,

Refrain

I'll buy me a fol - de - rol - dy,

til - de tol - dy, seek - a dou - ble roll,

Jen - nie Jen - kins, roll.

3. Will you wear purple, my dear, O my dear?
Oh, will you wear purple, Jennie Jenkins?
I won't wear purple, it's the color of a turtle,
Refrain

RIDING IN A BUGGY
TRADITIONAL FOLK SONG

S.B.900

COTTON NEEDS A-PICKING

SOUTHERN FOLK SONG

ELIZA JANE

KENTUCKY FOLK SONG

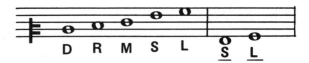

Lively

1. Stepped up - on   the   rail - road,   Thought we'd have   some rain;
2. Hear   the whis - tle   blow - ing,   Let's   get   on   the   train;

Get   your   old   blue bon - net;   Let's   go,   E - li - za
En - gine starts   a - groan - ing;   We're   off,   E - li - za

Refrain

Jane!
Jane!   Shoop - ee,   Li - za,   pret - ty   lit - tle   girl!

Shoop - ee,   Li - za   Jane!   Shoop - ee,   Li - za,

pret - ty   lit - tle   girl,   Let's   get   on   the   train!

BARNYARD SONG
ENGLISH FOLK SONG

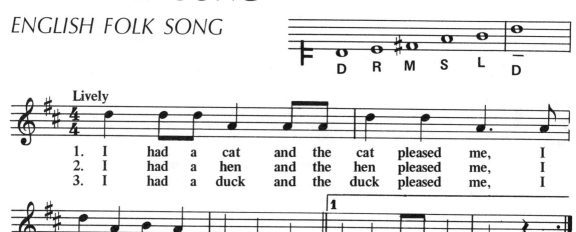

Lively

1. I had a cat and the cat pleased me, I
2. I had a hen and the hen pleased me, I
3. I had a duck and the duck pleased me, I

fed my cat by yon-der tree. Cat goes fid-dle dee fee
fed my hen by yon-der tree.
fed my duck by yon-der tree.

2-3   *3rd stanza only*

Hen goes chim-ny chuck   Cat goes fid-dle dee fee.
Duck goes quack, quack

FAREWELL, MY OWN TRUE LOVE
AMERICAN FOLK SONG

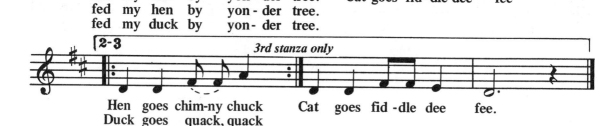

1. Fare well, my own true love, Fare -
2. Ten thou - sand mile my love, Through
3. Oh, don't you see that dove That

well a lit - tle while, I'm goin' a - way but I'll
Eng - land, France, and Spain; My rov - ing mind shall
flies from vine to vine. A - mourn - ing for his

come a - gain. If I go ten thou - sand mile.
nev - er rest Till I see your face a - gain.
own true love, Just as I will mourn for mine.

HOP UP, MY LADIES

AMERICAN FOLK SONG

Did you ev - er go to meet - ing, Un - cle

Joe, Un - cle Joe? Did you ev - er go to

meet - ing, Un - cle Joe? _____ Did you

ev - er go to meet - ing, Un - cle Joe, Un - cle Joe? Don't

mind the weath - er, so the winds don't blow.

Refrain

Hop up, my la - dies, three in a row;

Hop up, my la - dies, three in a row;

Hop, up, my la - dies, three in a row; Don't

mind the weath - er, so the winds don't blow!

S.B.900

DOWN IN THE MEADOW
SOUTHERN FOLK SONG

1. Down in the mead - ow, hop a doo - dle, hop a doo - dle,
2. Down in the barn - yard, hop a doo - dle, hop a doo - dle,

Down in the mead - ow, hop a doo - dle doo!
Down in the barn - yard, hop a doo - dle doo!

Down in the mead - ow the colt be - gan to prance, The
Down in the barn - yard, the goose be - gan to sing, The

cow be - gan to whis - tle, and the pig be - gan to dance.
hen be - gan to cack - le, as the roost - er flapped a wing.

FARE THEE WELL, MY HONEY
FOLK BLUES

1. Oh, some folks say that the blues ain't bad, It's the
2. If I had wings like — No - ah's dove, I'd fly

worst old feel-ing that I ev-er had. Fare thee well, my
up the riv-er to the one I love. Fare thee well, my

hon-ey, Fare thee well. _____
hon-ey, Fare thee well. _____

3. Oh, one of these days, and it won't be long.
You'll call my name and _ I'll be gone.
Fare thee well, my honey,
Fare thee well.

SOURWOOD MOUNTAIN

SOUTHERN FOLK SONG

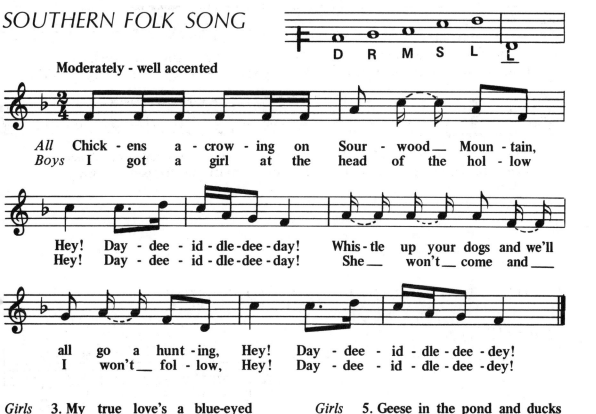

Moderately - well accented

All Chick-ens a-crow-ing on Sour-wood_ Moun-tain,
Boys I got a girl at the head of the hol-low

Hey! Day-dee-id-dle-dee-day! Whis-tle up your dogs and we'll
Hey! Day-dee-id-dle-dee-day! She_ won't_ come and _

all go a hunt-ing, Hey! Day-dee-id-dle-dee-dey!
I won't_ fol-low, Hey! Day-dee-id-dle-dee-dey!

Girls 3. My true love's a blue-eyed
daisy. Hey! etc.
If she doesn't love me, I'll go
crazy. Hey! etc.

Boys 4. My true love lives up the river,
Hey! etc.
Built a little boat just to be
with her. Hey! etc.

Girls 5. Geese in the pond and ducks
in the ocean. Hey! etc.
I'm going dancing when I take
a notion. Hey! etc.

All 6. You swing me and I'll swing
you, Hey! etc.
We'll go to heaven in the same
old shoe. Hey! etc.

S.B.900

THE RIDDLE SONG
AMERICAN FOLK SONG

1. I gave my love a cher-ry that has no stone; I
2. How can there be a cher-ry that has no stone? How
3. A cher-ry when it's bloom-ing, it has no stone; A

gave my love a chick-en that has no____ bone; I
can there be a chick-en that has no____ bone; How
chick-en when it's pip-ping, it has no____ bone; A

gave my love a ring____ that has no____ end; I
can there be a ring____ that has no____ end? How
ring ____ when it's roll-ing, it has no____ end; A

gave my love a ba-by, there's no cry-en.
can there be a ba-by, there's no cry-en?
ba-by when it's sleep-ing, there's no cry-en.

THE BIRDS' SONG
AMERICAN FOLK SONG

1. "Hi!" said the black-bird, sit-ing on a chair,
2. "Hi!" said the black-bird, talk-ing to a squirrel,
3. "Hi!" said the black-bird, as a-way he flew,

"Once I court - ed a la - dy fair;
"Once I court - ed a hand - some girl;
"Once I had not one girl but two;

She proved fick - le and turned her back, And
She proved fick - le and from me fled, And
One did -n't love me, the oth - er would, Now

ev - er since then I've dressed in black."
ev - er since then I've worn all red."
don't you all think my no - tion's good?"

Refrain

Row - dy, dow - dy, did -dle - o - dum,

Row - dy, dow - dy, did -dle - o - day;

Row - dy dow - dy, did -dle - o - dum,

Row - dy dow - dy, did -dle - o - day.

A LONG TIME AGO
AMERICAN FOLK SONG

Lively

1. A long time a - go, I re - mem - ber it well; A __
2. Now she had a boy - friend who close by did dwell; He was
3. And just at that mo - ment her fa - ther ap - peared; And __

lone in a poor - house, a maid - en did dwell; She
cross - eyed in both feet and hump - backed as well; Said
looked on his daugh - ter with eyes in his tears; He

lived with her fa - ther and __ moth - er se - rene; Her
he, "Let us fly by the __ light of yon star, For
seized the base vil - lain by the hand with his throat, And

age it was __ red and her hair was nine - teen.
you are the __ eye of my ap - ple, you are."
shot him with a horse pis - tol raised from a colt.

WHEN THE TRAIN COMES ALONG

AMERICAN FOLK SONG

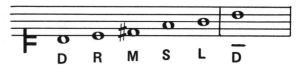

Lively
Refrain

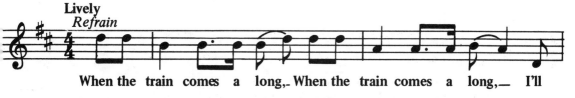

When the train comes a long,_ When the train comes a long,__ I'll

meet you at the sta - tion when the train comes a long.

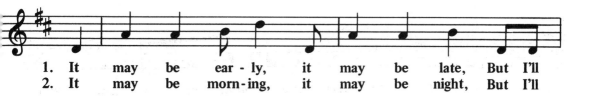

1. It may be ear - ly, it may be late, But I'll
2. It may be morn - ing, it may be night, But I'll

to Refrain

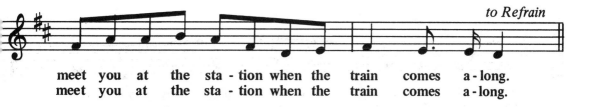

meet you at the sta - tion when the train comes a - long.
meet you at the sta - tion when the train comes a - long.

S.B.900

SOURWOOD MOUNTAIN
SOUTHERN FOLK SONG

OLD BALD EAGLE

APPALACHIAN MOUNTAIN
SONG

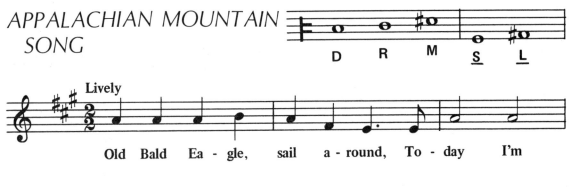

Old Bald Ea - gle, sail a - round, To - day I'm

gone; Old Bald Ea - gle, sail a - round, To - day I'm

gone. Sail a - round the moun - tain - top!

Sail a - round, I say! Sail a - round the

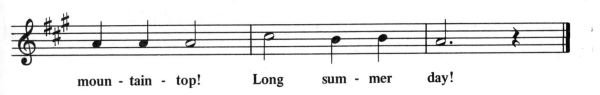

moun - tain - top! Long sum - mer day!

S.B.900

OLE TARE RIVER
AMERICAN FOLK SONG

Brightly

1. Way_____ down in North Car - 'li - na,
2. Now,_____ Nan - cy, I must leave you,

(whistle)_____

On the banks of
Do not let our

Ole Tare Riv - er, (whistle)_____

part - ing grieve you,

I go from there to Al - a - bam - a, (whistle)_____

Dance and ___ sing, for - get your sor-row,

_____

For to see my ole Aunt Han - nah.
I'll be back some - time to - mor-row.

(whistle)_____

THE MEEK OLD CROW

AMERICAN FOLK SONG

Ballad Style

1. "Come!" said his wife — to the meek old crow,
2. "Now", said the swal-low, sit - ting on a barn,
3. "Who", said the owl — with — great round eyes,

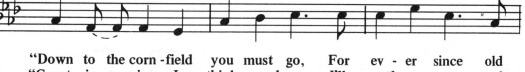

"Down to the corn -field you must go, For ev - er since old
"Court - ing — is I think, no harm. I'll smooth my wrongs and
"Does not — think that I am wise? The rea - son why I

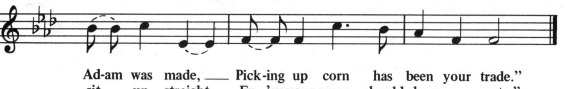

Ad-am was made, — Pick-ing up corn has been your trade."
sit — up straight. — Ev -'ry young man should choose a mate."
fly — by night Is seek - ing for my hearts de - light."

4. "Fie," said the woodpecker, sitting
   on the fence,
   "Once I courted a handsome wench;
   She turned fickle and from me fled.
   Ever since then my head's been red."

5. "Ah!" said the blackbird, sitting on a
   tree
   "Once I courted a fair ladye.
   She was proud and turned her back.
   From that day I've dressed in black."

6. "Well," said the little turtledove,
   "If I had a mind to win my love,
   I'd court her night, I'd court her
   day,
   Never give her time to say me nay."

7. "Hi!" said the bluejay as she flew,
   "If I were a young man, I'd have two.
   If one prove false and chance for to
   go,
   I'd have a new string to my bow."

S.B.900

GOING DOWN TO CAIRO
AMERICAN FOLK SONG

Go - ing down to Cai - ro, good - bye and a bye - bye,
(Kā' - ro)

Go - ing down to Cai - ro, good - bye, Li - za Jane.

Mop that deck and make it shine, good - bye and a bye - bye;

Mop that deck and make it shine, good - bye, Li - za Jane.

BLACK SHEEP
AMERICAN FOLK SONG

Black sheep, black sheep, where'd you leave your lamb?

'Way o - ver in the val - ley. The

SCOTLAND'S BURNING
TRADITIONAL ROUND

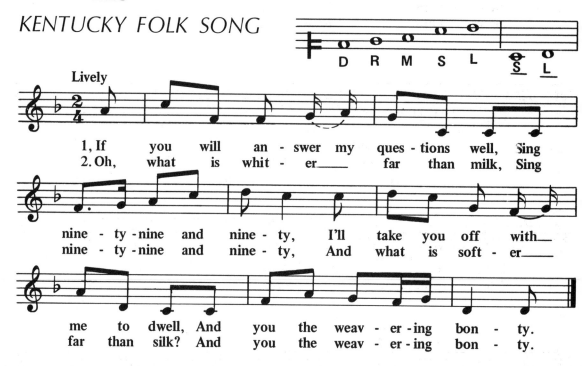

Moderately

Scot-land's burn-ing, Scot-land's burn-ing, Look out, look out.

Fire, fire, fire, fire, Pour on wa-ter, pour on wa-ter!

RIDDLES
KENTUCKY FOLK SONG

Lively

1, If you will an - swer my ques - tions well, Sing
2. Oh, what is whit - er_____ far than milk, Sing

nine - ty -nine and nine-ty, I'll take you off with___
nine - ty -nine and nine-ty, And what is soft - er_____

me to dwell, And you the weav - er -ing bon - ty.
far than silk? And you the weav - er -ing bon - ty.

3. Oh, snow is whiter far than milk, . . .
   And down is softer far than silk. . . .

4. Oh, what is louder than a horn? . . .
   And what is sharper than a thorn? . . .

5. Oh, thunder's louder than a horn, . . .
   And lighting's sharper than a thorn, . . .

6. Oh, what red fruit September grows? . . .
   And what thing round the whole
   world goes? . . .

7. The apple in September grows, . . .
   And air around the whole world goes, . . .

8. Oh, you have answered my questions
   well, . . .
   I'll take you off with me to dwell.

MINGO MOUNTAIN

KENTUCKY FOLK SONG

Slowly

1. I've been trav - 'lin' o - ver these
2. Ain't no ham - mer on_____ these

moun - tains For - ty long years,
moun - tains Rings_____ like mine,

for - ty long years. I'm goin'
rings_____ like mine. This old

back to_____ the Min - go moun - tains,
ham - mer_____ it rings like sil - ver,

That's my home, that's my home._____
Shines like gold, shines like gold._____

THE NIGHTINGALE
KENTUCKY FOLK SONG

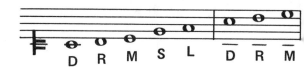

Smoothly

1. One morn-ing, one morn-ing, one morn-ing in May, I
2. "Good morn-ing, good morn-ing, good morn-ing to thee, O

met a fair cou - ple a - mak - ing their way, And
where are you go - ing, my pret - ty la - dy?" O

one was a la - dy so neat and so fair, The
I am a goin' to the banks of the sea, To

oth - er a sol - dier, a brave vol - un - teer.
hear ___ the night - in - gale sing ___ for me."

3. We hadn't been standing but one hour or two,
   When from his knapsack a fiddle he drew,
   The tune that he played made the valleys ring
   With sounds such as nightingales surely would sing.

4. "O lady, fair lady, it's time to return."
   "No, wait, for another tune do I yearn,
   I'd much rather hear just a tune on one string,
   Than all of the songs that the nightingales sing."

STEAL AWAY

SPIRITUAL

Slowly
Refrain

Steal a -way, steal a-way, steal a-way to Je - sus. Steal a -way, steal a-way home, I ain't got long to stay here.

Faster
Solo

1. My Lord_____
2. Green trees_____ are
3. My Lord_____

Chorus

calls me, He calls me by the thun-der; The trum-pet sounds with -
bend-ing; Poor sin - ners stand a - trem-bling; The trum-pet sounds with -
calls me, He calls me by the light-ning; The trum-pet sounds with -

in - a my soul; I ain't got long to stay here.
in - a my soul; I ain't got long to stay here.
in - a my soul; I ain't got long to stay here.

S.B.900

EZEKIEL SAW THE WHEEL

SPIRITUAL

Lightly
Refrain

E - ze - kiel saw the wheel, 'Way up in the

mid - dle of the air; E - ze - kiel saw the wheel,

'Way in the mid - dle of the air; The

big wheel runs by faith, Lit - tle wheel runs by the

grace of God, A wheel in a wheel,

'Way in the mid - dle of the air.

1. I'll tell you what a hyp - o - crite - 'll do,
2. E - ze - kiel saw the wheel ___ of ___ time,

'Way in the mid - dle of the air;
'Way in the mid - dle of the air;

S.B.900

He'll talk a - bout me and he'll talk a - bout you,
And ev - 'ry spoke was_____ hu - man - kind,

to Refrain

'Way in the mid - dle of the air.
'Way in the mid - dle of the air.

BUTTON, YOU MUST WANDER
AMERICAN GAME SONG

D R M S L

Moderately

But - ton, you must wan - der, wan - der,

wan - der; But - ton, you must wan - der

ev - 'ry - where. Bright eyes will find you;

Sharp eyes will find you; But - ton, you must

wan - der ev - 'ry - where.

TWO WINGS
SPIRITUAL

D   R   M   S   L   D

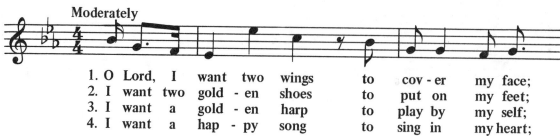

1. O Lord, I want two wings to cov-er my face;
2. I want two gold-en shoes to put on my feet;
3. I want a gold-en harp to play by my self;
4. I want a hap-py song to sing in my heart;

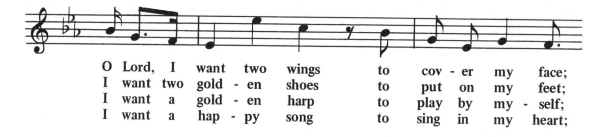

O Lord, I want two wings to cov-er my face;
I want two gold-en shoes to put on my feet;
I want a gold-en harp to play by my-self;
I want a hap-py song to sing in my heart;

O Lord, I want two wings to cov-er my face;
I want two gold-en shoes to put on my feet;
I want a gold-en harp to play by my-self;
I want a hap-py song to sing in my heart;

And the world can do me no harm.
And the world can do me no harm.
And the world can do me no harm.
And the world can do me no harm.

WAYFARING STRANGER

FOLK SONG

I'm just a poor way-far-ing stran-ger A trav-'ling thro' this world of woe; But there's no sick-ness, toil, nor dan-ger In that bright world to which I go; I'm go-ing there to see my fa-ther, I'm go-ing
(mother)
(brother)
there no more to roam, I'm just a-go-ing o-ver Jor-dan, I'm just a-go-ing o-ver home.

S.B.900

THERE'S A LITTLE WHEEL

SPIRITUAL

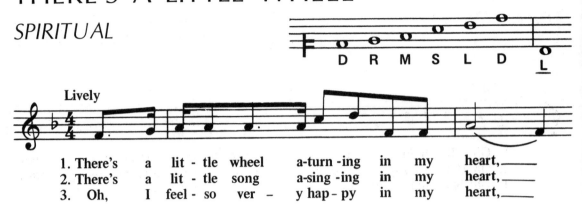

1. There's a lit - tle wheel a-turn-ing in my heart,_____
2. There's a lit - tle song a-sing-ing in my heart,_____
3. Oh, I feel - so ver – y hap - py in my heart,_____

There's a lit -tle wheel a - turn - ing in my heart,
There's a lit -tle song a - sing - ing in my heart,
Oh, I feel so ver - y hap - py in my heart,

In my heart, _____ in my heart, _____ There's a
In my heart, _____ in my heart, _____ There's a
In my heart, _____ in my heart, _____ Oh, I

lit - tle wheel a - turn - ing in my heart.
lit - tle song a - sing - ing in my heart.
feel so ver – y hap - py in my heart.

GO 'WAY, OLD MAN

FOLK SONG

D   R   M   S   L

Lively

1. Oh! I'll build me a lit - tle hut, In the moun-tains so high,
2. Oh! Her eyes sparkle like the di - a-mond, Like the bright morn-ing star,
3. Oh! She does not look so sweet Like the rose on the vine,

I will gaze on my true love, As she pass - es by!
Oh Her cheeks are so love - ly, Her face is so fa'r!
Long live that love - ly la - dy That dwells in my mind!

Refrain

Go 'way, old man _____, and leave me a - lone,

For I am a stran - ger, and a - long way from home!

S.B.900

MICHAEL, ROW THE BOAT ASHORE

SPIRITUAL

With feeling

1. Mi - chael, row the boat a - shore, Hal - le
2. Mi - chael's boat's a mu - sic boat, Hal - le

lu - jah! Mi - chael, row the boat a
lu - jah! Mi - chael's boat's a mu - sic

shore, Hal - le lu - jah!
boat, Hal - le lu - jah!

3. Michael, row the boat ashore, Hallelujah! (2 times)
4. Sister, help to trim the sail, Hallelujah! (2 times)
5. Michael, row the boat ashore, Hallelujah! (2 times)

TRAIN IS A-COMING

SPIRITUAL

Moderately

Fine

1. Train___ is a - com - ing, Oh, yes,
2. Bet - ter get your tick - et, Oh, yes,
3. Train___ is a - leav - ing, Oh, yes,

Train___ is a - com - ing,___ Oh, yes,
Bet - ter get your tick - et,___ Oh, yes,
Train___ is a - leav - ing,___ Oh, yes,

D.C. al Fine

Train___ is a - com - ing, Train _ is a - com - ing,
Bet - ter get your tick - et, Bet - ter get your tick - et,
Train___ is a - com - ing, Train _ is a - leav - ing,

THE GOSPEL TRAIN

SPIRITUAL

Happily

1. The gos - pel train is com - ing, ____ I
2. I hear the bell and whis - tle, ____ She's
3. No sig - nal from an - oth - er train To

hear it just at hand, I hear the car wheels
com - ing round the curve, She's play - ing all her
fol - low on the line, O sin - ner, you're for -

mov - ing ____ And rum - bling through the land. ____
steam and pow'r And strain - ing ev - 'ry nerve. ____
ev - er lost If once you're left be - hind. ____

Refrain

Get on board, lit - tle chil - dren, Get on board, lit - tle

chil - dren, Get on board, lit - tle chil - dren For there's

1 **2**

room for man - y a - more. more.

4. She's nearing now the station,
O Sinner, don't be vain,
But come and get your ticket
And be ready for the train
Refrain

5. We soon will reach the station,
Oh, how we then shall sing.
With all the heavenly army
We'll make the welkin ring.
Refrain

FISHPOLE SONG
SOUTHERN SINGING GAME

1. Who's got a fish-pole? We do!
2. Who's got a fish-line? We do!

Who's got a fish-pole? We do! Who's got a fish-pole?
Who's got a fish-line? We do! Who's got a fish-line?

We do! Fish-pole needs a line.
We do! Fish-line needs a hook.

3. Who's got a fish-hook? We do!
Who's got a fish-hook? We do!
Who's got a fish-hook? We do!
Fish-hook needs some bait.

4. Who's got a cricket? We do!
Who's got a cricket? We do!
Who's got a cricket? We do!
Cricket catch a fish!

THE ANGEL BAND
SPIRITUAL

There was one, there were two, there were three lit-tle

an-gels, There were four, there were five, there were six lit-tle

S.B.900

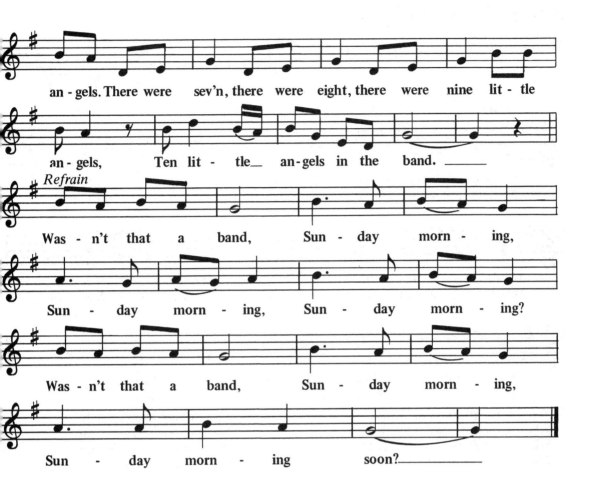

an - gels. There were sev'n, there were eight, there were nine lit - tle

an - gels, Ten lit - tle_ an - gels in the band. _____

Refrain

Was - n't that a band, Sun - day morn - ing,

Sun - day morn - ing, Sun - day morn - ing?

Was - n't that a band, Sun - day morn - ing,

Sun - day morn - ing soon?_____

DE BEZEM (The Broom)

DUTCH ROUND

Lively

De be - zem, de be - zem, Wat
Pronounced: *Deh bay - zehm, deh bay - zehm, Vaht*

doe je er mee? Wat doe je er mee? Wij ve - gen er mee, Wij
doo yeh ehr may? Vaht doo yeh ehr may? Vee feh - gehn ehr may, Vee

ve - gen er mee, De vloer aan, de vloer aan!
feh - gehn ehr may, Deh fleur ahn, deh fleur ahn!

S.B.900

SWING LOW, SWEET CHARIOT

SPIRITUAL

Moderately
Refrain

Swing low, sweet char - i ot, ___ Com-ing for to car-ry me

home, Swing low, sweet char - i - ot, ___

Com - ing for to car - ry me home.

1. I looked o - ver Jor - dan and what did I see, ___
2. If you get ___ there ___ be - fore ___ I do, ___
3. I'm some - times ___ up ___ and some - times down, ___

Com - ing for to car - ry me home, A
Com - ing for to car - ry me home, Just
Com - ing for to car - ry me home, But

band ___ of an - gels com - ing af - ter me, ___
tell ___ my friends I'm com - ing ___ too, ___
still ___ my soul feels heav - en - ly ___ bound, ___

to Refrain

Com - ing for to car - ry me home.
Com - ing for to car - ry me home.
Com - ing for to car - ry me home.

THE OLD ARK
SPIRITUAL

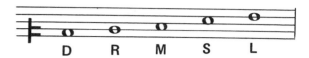

Moderately

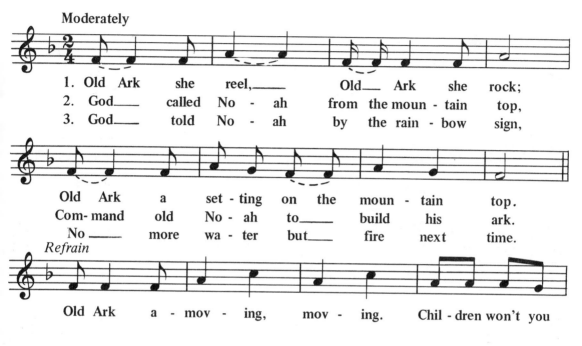

1. Old Ark she reel,___ Old___ Ark she rock;
2. God___ called No - ah from the moun - tain top,
3. God___ told No - ah by the rain - bow sign,

Old Ark a set - ting on the moun - tain top.
Com- mand old No - ah to___ build his ark.
No___ more wa - ter but___ fire next time.

Refrain

Old Ark a - mov - ing, mov - ing. Chil - dren won't you

come a - long? Old Ark a - mov - ing, I thank God!

Old Ark she reel, Old Ark she rock;

Old Ark a - set - ting on the moun - tain top.

S.B.900

OH, WON'T YOU SIT DOWN?

SPIRITUAL

Rhythmically
Refrain

Oh, won't you sit down?__ Lord, I

can't sit down.__ Oh, won't you sit down? Lord, I

can't sit down.__ Oh, won't you sit down? Lord, I

can't sit down__ 'Cause I just got to Heav-en, Goin' to

look a-round. 1.Who's that yon-der dressed in red?__
                2.Who's that yon-der dressed in blue?__

Must be the chil-dren that old Mo-ses led. _ Who's that yon-der
Must be the chil-dren that are com-ing through. Who's that yon-der

dressed in white? Must be the chil-dren of the Is-rael-ite.__
dressed in black? Must be the hyp-o-crites a-turn-in' back.__

S.B.900

LONESOME VALLEY

SPIRITUAL

Reverently

1. Je - sus walked_____ this lone - some val - ley,_____ He had to walk_____ it by Him - self, Oh, no - bod - y else_____ could walk it for Him._____ He had to walk it for_____ Him - self._____

2. We must walk_____ this lone - some val - ley,_____ We have to walk_____ it by our - selves, Oh, no - bod - y else_____ can walk it for us._____ We have to walk it for_____ our - selves._____

3. You must go_____ and stand your tri - al,_____ You have to stand_____ it by your - self, O, no - bod - y else_____ can stand it for you._____ You have to stand it for_____ your - self._____

S.B.900

EV'RY TIME I FEEL THE SPIRIT

SPIRITUAL

S.B.900

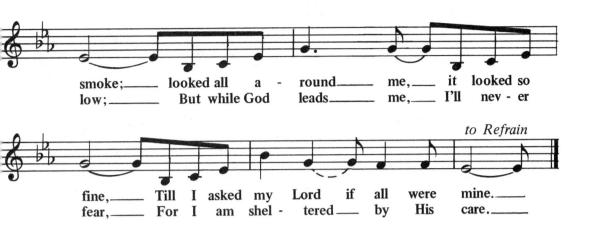

smoke;_____ looked all a - round_____ me,____ it looked so

low;_____ But while God leads_____ me,____ I'll nev - er

to Refrain

fine,____ Till I asked my Lord if all were mine.____

fear,____ For I am shel - tered____ by His care.____

NEVER SLEEP LATE ANY MORE

FOLK SONG

Brightly

Oh, just let me get up in the ear - ly morn,

Just let me get up in the ear - ly morn,

Just let me get up in the ear - ly morn And I'll

nev - er sleep late an - y more._____

66

MARY HAD A BABY

SPIRITUAL

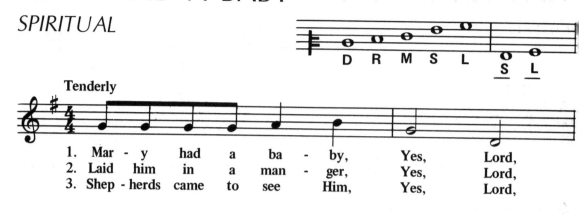

Tenderly

1. Mar - y had a ba - by, Yes, Lord,
2. Laid him in a man - ger, Yes, Lord,
3. Shep - herds came to see Him, Yes, Lord,

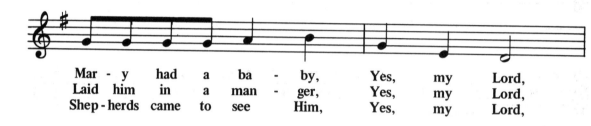

Mar - y had a ba - by, Yes, my Lord,
Laid him in a man - ger, Yes, my Lord,
Shep - herds came to see Him, Yes, my Lord,

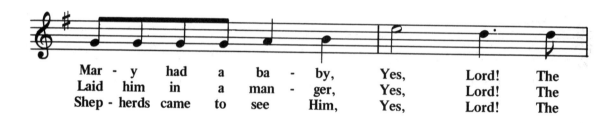

Mar - y had a ba - by, Yes, Lord! The
Laid him in a man - ger, Yes, Lord! The
Shep - herds came to see Him, Yes, Lord! The

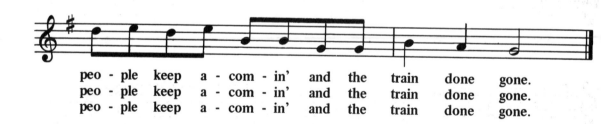

peo - ple keep a - com - in' and the train done gone.
peo - ple keep a - com - in' and the train done gone.
peo - ple keep a - com - in' and the train done gone.

NOW LET ME FLY

SPIRITUAL

Moderately

Now let me fly,_____ Now let me fly,_____

_____ Now let me fly__ way up high,__

Fine

Way in the mid - dle of the air.

Verse

Way down yon - der in the mid - dle of the field,

See me work - ing at the char - iot wheel.

Not so par - tic - 'lar 'bout work - ing at the wheel,

D.C. al Fine

But I just want to see how the char - iot feels.

S.B.900

CHATTER WITH THE ANGELS

SPIRITUAL

I hope to join that band and chat-ter with the an-gels all day long!

YOU SHALL REAP

SPIRITUAL

You shall reap___ just what you sow, You shall reap what you sow; On the moun - tain, in the val - ley,___ You shall reap___ just what you sow. Broth - er, you shall sow.

70

ALL NIGHT, ALL DAY

SPIRITUAL

THE RAILROAD CORRAL

COWBOY SONG

Moderately

1. We're up in the morn - ing ere break - ing of
2. Come take up your cinch - es, come shake out your

day, The chuck wag - on's bus - y, the
reins, Come wake your old bron - co and

flap - jack's in play. The herd is a
break for the plains: Come roust out your

stir o - ver hill - side and vale, With the
steers from the long chap - ar - ral, For the

night rid - ers crowd - ing them in - to the trail.
out - fit is off to the rail - road cor - ral.

3. The afternoon shadows are startin' to lean
   When the chuck wagon sticks in the marshy ravine;
   The herds scatter farther than vision can look,
   You can bet all true punchers will help out the cook.

4. The longest of days must reach evening at last,
   The mountains all climbed and the creeks all are past;
   The herd is a-drooping and fast falls the night,
   Let them droop if they will, for the railroad's in sight!

NIGHT HERDING SONG

COWBOY SONG

GOODBYE, OL' PAINT
COWBOY SONG

Moderately
Refrain

Good - bye, ol' Paint, I'm a - leav - in' Chey -

enne, Good - bye, ol' Paint, I'm a - leav - in' Chey - enne.

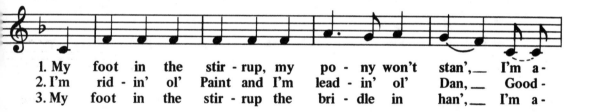

1. My foot in the stir - rup, my po - ny won't stan', __ I'm a -
2. I'm rid - in' ol' Paint and I'm lead - in' ol' Dan, __ Good -
3. My foot in the stir - rup the bri - dle in han', __ I'm a -

to Refrain

leav - in' Chey - enne an' I'm off for Mon - tan'. __
bye, lit - tle An - nie, I'm off for Mon - tan'. __
leav - in' Chey - enne an' I'm off for Mon - tan'. __

. B.900

THE COLORADO TRAIL

COWBOY SONG

DONEY GAL

COWBOY SONG

Slowly

We're a - lone, Do - ney Gal, in the wind and hail;_____ Got to drive those____ do - gies____ down the trail._____

1. We'll ride the range from sun to sun, For a cow - boy's work is____ nev - er done; He's up and gone at the break of day, Driv - in' the do - gies on their wea - ry way.

2. A cow - boy's life is a wea - ry thing, For its Rope____ and brand and____ ride and sing Yes, day or night, in the rain or hail, He'll stay with his do - gies out____ on the trail.

WHOO-PEE TI YI YO!

COWBOY SONG

As I was a-walk-ing one morn-ing for pleas-ure, I met a cow-punch-er a-rid-ing a-long, His hat was thrown back and his spurs were a-jin-gling, And as he ap-proached, he was sing-ing this song. Whoo-pee ti yi yo!__ Git a-long, lit-tle do-gies, It's your mis-for-tune and none of my own, Whoo-pee ti yi yo!__ Git a-long, lit-tle do-gies, You know that Wy-o-ming will be your new home.

S.B.900